Prayers
of
Praise
&
Celebration

Douglas Knighton

"For your progress & joy in the faith."
Doug

Copyright © 2016 Douglas Knighton

All rights reserved.

ISBN: 978-1539661153

This work is licensed under

the Creative Commons

Attribution-NonCommercial-NoDerivs 3.0 Unported License.

To view a copy of this license, visit

http://creativecommons.org/licenses/by-nc-nd/3.0/

or send a letter to:

Creative Commons

171 Second Street, Suite 300

San Francisco, California 94105

USA

Scripture quotations taken from the
New American Standard Bible®,
Copyright © 1960, 1962, 1963, 1968, 1971, 1972, 1973,
1975, 1977, 1995 by The Lockman Foundation
Used by permission. (www.Lockman.org)

Preface

In the mid '70s, Bruce Leafblad, the lead musician at Lake Avenue Church in Pasadena, made a significant change in the format of the Sunday morning service. Each service began with one of the pastors leading the congregation in a prayer of praise. Remarkably, none of these prayers ever used the word "praise." Instead, they articulated the beauty of the character of God and the marvels of his works, so that God would know how much we appreciated him and how much we were impressed by what he was doing. I loved these prayers. I loved the power and majesty celebrated in them. When I was able to begin holding worship services for the 434th Air Refueling Wing at Grissom Air Force Base in 1988, I used this format with great joy. Later, as I was planning how to format the "Promises for the Battle" devotional series, it seemed appropriate to include a prayer of praise as a companion to the didactic material. So the first thirty two pages of this volume recapitulate the prayers which accompanied each series of meditations.

Somewhere in the early 80's I was appointed the official prayer giver for the Thanksgiving and Christmas family meals. As I contemplated what to say, I had an idea: Why not write a poem, specifically a sonnet? It only took about four hours to write the first one, as I recall. I enjoyed the effort and liked the result. So I maintained the practice until it became a tradition. Some of them are reformulations of specific scriptures (these are noted under the titles where this occurred). Others are simply reflections on the generosity of God and the gratitude of my heart. While the Thanksgiving sonnets combine praise and gratitude, the Christmas sonnets celebrate the various aspects and implications of the incarnation, mostly falling into the category of praise.

My prayer for you is that my words will become your words so we can join one another as we celebrate and praise our God.

Doug Knighton
October, 2016, Edmonds WA.

Praised Abundance

They shall speak of the power of your awesome acts; and tell of your greatness. They shall bubble over with the memory of your abundant goodness, singing joyfully of your righteousness. Psalms 145:7

From idol worship to Father of Many Nations, you transformed Abraham into the "Friend of God." You guided the children of promise through family quarrels and Pharaoh's conquest. According to your purpose to glorify yourself in your people, you kept seven thousand from worshiping Baal. And you restored a nation from the punishment of captivity, so the Messianic line could continue until Jesus appeared in the fullness of time. From the palaces of Heaven you sent your Son to suffer shame and pain and death so I could be redeemed from sin's dread grasp, released from the need to glory in my own achievements, enabled to boast in your overwhelming compassion, mercy and grace. As with Joseph, you worked to turn others' evil intentions into good for me. As with David, you defeated those who tried to keep me from your plans for my life. As with Josiah, you brought me back to your word. As with Habakkuk, you overcame my cynical heart through your sovereign power. As with Peter, you brought me back from failures in faith. You have satisfied my soul with your goodness, with an abundance of peace and truth. Amen.

Well-Watched Praise

The Eternal is in his holy temple; the Eternal's throne is in heaven. His eyes watch; his eyes examine all people. The Eternal tests for righteousness; indeed he hates wickedness and the love of violence. Psalm 11:4–5

Eternal God, as you scan and scrutinize our lives from the beauty and majesty of your heavenly dwelling, we trust in your integrity and fairness. We cannot turn your head or twist your arm; you do not show partiality or take a bribe. You neither condemn the just nor condone the unjust. Your values are certain and your evaluation of us clear. When we persevere as our confidence in you is tested, you approve; for such righteousness honors your holiness: your infinite, unexcelled and irreplaceable worth. When we respond to difficult situations and defiant people in gentle ways which accord with your design, in ways which correspond to our task to extend your gracious goodness to the world around us, your joyous approval flows from your heart. When Enoch walked in close fellowship with you, you were so pleased you took him to yourself. When Abraham demonstrated his faith through obedience, you approved. When Rahab hid the Israeli spies, you approved of her faith. When Jesus went to the cross, you showed your approval by raising him from the grave. This consistent commitment to love those who demonstrate a delight in your goodness gives us hope and encourages us to consistently commit ourselves to the same end; for we know that no good deed goes unnoticed by your all-seeing eyes. Amen.

Comforted Praise

The Eternal has comforted his people. He has redeemed Jerusalem. The Eternal has bared his holy arm In the sight of all the nations, that all the ends of the earth may see the salvation of our God. Isaiah 52:9–10

On a hill far away, on an old, rugged cross, you comforted me, O God. In full view of the nations of earth, the Lamb of God took away the sin of his brothers and sisters from every tribe and tongue and people and nation. I may not have felt comforted at the time, but when I realized what you did in Jesus' life, death and resurrection, when I realized how wonderful my fellowship with you would be through my relationship with him, my soul was restored and joy filled my heart. Now, in Jesus' name you continually display your holy strength on my behalf, delivering me daily from the attacks of Satan, taking away my fear of any lasting harm he can do. Your peace and well-being give me courage to continue to fight the fight of faith. "Though I walk through the valley of the shadow of death, I will fear no evil. You are with me and your rod and your staff comfort me." For I know that the "holy arm" that rescued me from your wrath will defend and protect and sustain me until my salvation is completed when Jesus returns in the sight of all the nations. O holy Comforter, the river of your peace flows alongside my path. It is well with my soul. Amen

Glorious Answers

Call upon me in the day of trouble; I shall rescue you, and you will honor me. Psalm 50:15

Because of my love for you, O God, you delivered me. Because I knew your reputation, you set me securely in a place of refuge. As I walked through the valley of the shadow of death, you were with me. In every trouble you have been present. There is no God beside you. You alone work for those who call on you and wait patiently for you. In your mercy you stooped to my weakness, tenderly, patiently supplying the wisdom and power I lack, so I pursued your desires for my life. Your Spirit even augmented my prayers with intensely fervent groanings of his own, having felt the deepest desires of my heart and matched them to those of yours. The fruit of loving, joyful, obedience burst forth on the branch of my life, a fitting tribute to your gracious work. Because of Jesus you forgive my sin, restore our fellowship, enable my humility, overcome my timidity, and give me the gifts I need for ministry, when I call out to you. Your answers are always more than generous, more than faithful, more than I imagine I'll need. How satisfying it is to behold your salvation as you draw me nearer and nearer through the mercy and grace that flow from your throne as I draw near to you in prayer! Forever amen.

Pardoning Praise

You shall not hate your brother in your heart; ... you shall not take vengeance, nor bear any grudge ... but you shall love your neighbor as yourself; for I am Yahweh ... who brought you out of the land of Egypt. Leviticus 19:17–18

Mercy, grace and peace are gifts from you, O God, which I cherish especially because of what you have done to make them mine. Just as you brought the Children of Israel out of bondage in Egypt with mighty works, so you have delivered me from my bondage to sin and from the threat it held against my happiness. "There is no condemnation to those who are in Christ Jesus." So I love the mercy I have received from you. Even more, I cherish the freedom that comes with my forgiveness, especially the freedom from having to insure my own vengeance and vindication. Especially when others have caused me pain, I cherish the freedom to restore the relationship because of what Jesus did at Calvary. What a joy it is to know that judgment and justice are safe in your hands! What a joy it is to be relieved of that terrible burden, so that I can be free to extend your grace even to my enemies! Thank you, O Most Merciful, for the privilege of participating in the dispensation of your forgiving love, by the power of your Spirit, in the Name of Jesus. Amen & Amen!

Freedom that Praises

Thanks be to God that though you were slaves of sin, you became obedient from the heart to that form of teaching to which you were committed, and having been freed from sin, you became slaves of righteousness. Romans 6:17–18

Liberating Lord, I have never felt so free as in being bound to you. When I was enslaved to my commitment to self-sufficiency and self-exaltation, I had only a terrible prospect of suffering your wrath. For the wages of sin is death. I didn't even know it; so I was bound by ignorance as well as iniquity. Now, having been freed from my sin, I can enjoy the freedom of being enslaved to you. Commitment to entrust my future to you frees me from the fear of bearing that burden on my own. Seeing your rules for life as the best way to live frees me to experience the joy of your approval and blessing. Following you in the obedience of faith frees me to be of benefit to people everywhere. What's more amazing is that being enslaved to you, as I live righteously before you, gives me access to your presence. Because of my commitment to you, you are committed to allow me to enter with the saints and angels for worship, adoration and praise. How blessed am I, O God who made heaven and earth, who keeps faith forever, and who sets the prisoner free with the gift of eternal life! Amen.

Forgiven Praise

If you should mark iniquities, O Lord, who could stand? But there is forgiveness with you, that you might be feared. Psalm 130:3–4

Everything you do, Heavenly Father, shows me how magnificent you are! Forgiving me does not make you appear weak. It shows your great wisdom and power. For you devised a righteous way to overcome all the obstacles to your desire to do me good. Then you sent your beloved Son into the world to take on himself the wrath that should have been mine. Now, because of your delight in the love he showed for your glory, you pardon all who come to you in his name. What a comfort it is to know how intense your love for me will be, now that you have cleared a way to do me good with your whole heart and soul! What an encouragement your forgiveness is to pursue the fullness of joy a relationship with you could bring! What a delight it is to experience the unsearchable love of the of the God from whom I deserved unquenchable hate! There is no God like you, "who pardons iniquity and passes over the rebellion of the remnant of his possession; who does not retain his anger forever, because he delights in gracious love." How eagerly I await the Lord Jesus who offered himself for the sins of many, and who will return with the salvation he righteously purchased with his blood for people from every tribe, tongue, society and nation. Amen.

Praised By Perseverance

Blessed be the God and Father of our Lord Jesus Christ, who according to his great mercy has caused us to be born again ... and who protects us by his power through faith for a salvation ready to be revealed in the last time. 1 Peter 1:3–5

How precious is the hope you have given me, O God. You began a good work in me and you have promised to complete it. You will not withhold your compassion from me; your extravagant kindness and your truth will continually preserve me. Nothing can separate me from the love you show me in Christ Jesus, and you have proved this repeatedly. I remember how you kept Abraham and Moses and Joshua and Hannah and David and Isaiah and Habakkuk and Mary and Peter and John and Paul through the difficult days of their lives. What an encouragement their stories are! By your power their faith did not fail. Hoping against hope they rested in you, and you gave them perseverance. How wonderful it is to be part of those for whom Jesus suffered and died, part of all he redeemed from every tribe and tongue and people and nation, who definitely and assuredly will worship you, because those whom he justified, he also glorified. Because I am crucified with Christ according to your will, I can live by faith in him who loved me and gave himself for me forever. Amen.

Encouraged Praise

If the Eternal had not been my help, my soul would soon have dwelt in silence. If I should say, "My foot has slipped," your extravagant kindness, O Eternal, will hold me up. When my anxious thoughts multiply within me, your consolations delight my soul. Psalm 94:17–19

O Lord, how often have I felt like Jehoshaphat in face of the armies of Ammon and Moab, when he cried, "We are powerless before this great multitude, nor do we know what to do, but our eyes are on you." And how often you have consoled my soul by powerfully working on my behalf. Thank you for the memory of Scripture in which I see evidence of your loving salvation in situations far worse than mine. Thank you for bringing to mind the countless times you have filled my cup to overflowing and spread a table before me in the presence of my enemies. In the seemingly most hopeless situations you gave me reason to sing: "Fresh courage take; the clouds you so much dread are big with mercy, and shall break with blessings on your head!." The surprises of your mercy overcame every anxious thought. Who is like you, O Lord? There is no Rock besides you; no Creator, Redeemer, Defender, Protector, who has proved himself repeatedly as the only sovereign source of security and stability and freedom in a changing and uncertain world. Amen.

Contented Praise

Because your extravagant kindness is better than life, my lips will praise you. So I will bless you as long as I live. I will lift up my hands to your name. My soul is satisfied as with marrow and fatness, and my mouth offers praises with joyful lips. Psalm 63:3–5

O Glorious God, though the whole realm of nature were mine, I could not be satisfied. Even if I were the ruler of all the kingdoms of the earth, I could not be satisfied. For you alone satisfy. But I would be content with anything. For the generous, extravagant outpouring of your joyful goodness into my life is better than life itself. With me you have earned a reputation for being holy. You have filled my heart with your infinite, unexcelled and irreplaceable worth. I want no more than the fellowship of Heaven that is mine as I have Jesus as my saving Lord. I want no more than the love of Heaven that is mine as the Holy Spirit pours out the love of God in my heart. I want no more than the promise of your eternally showing me the surpassing riches of your grace. I want no more than being filled with all the fullness of God. With the assurance of your wise and powerful presence, I can be relaxed and comfortable and joyful and grateful in every circumstance. With the experience of your gracious providence, my heart is at rest as I perceive you in all your work for me in Jesus' name. Amen.

Praised By Godliness

Know that the Eternal has set apart the godly man for himself. The Eternal hears when I call to him. Psalm 4:3

Before any of my days began, O Lord, you had ordained them all and written them in your book. This was no whim, nor capricious contingency. I am a thread in your tapestry, not a piece of lint on your sleeve. You oversaw the genetic dispersions and conglomerations that would lead to my parents and to me. Through storm and earthquake and plague and war, through family squabbles and governmental bumbling, you guided history's course until the moment you chose to bring me into your picture. Timing, location, culture; nothing left to chance. How exquisitely precise! How magnificently complex! But more than just include me, you chose me, setting me apart to have fellowship with you forever. You sent your Son to die in my place so you could turn me from an ungodly, insulting individual into a person who will enjoy you and be a source of praise throughout eternity. By the power of your Spirit you are purging my heart of the fear and pride which keep me from fully appreciating how holy you are, so that one day I will be fit to dwell in your presence, ready to experience all the fullness of God. How utterly gracious! How totally benevolent! How wonderfully merciful! How amazingly glorious! Amen and amen!

Praising Holiness

Holy, Holy, Holy, is the Lord of the Universe, the fullness of the earth is his glory. Isaiah 6:3

Who is like you, having infinite, unexcelled and irreplaceable worth? O Eternal God, how I delight to consider the ways you manifest this value in the extravagance of your creation. For when I do, I realize again the magnitude of your holiness. Where simple function would have served, you made complex, integrated designs. Where one or two kinds would have sufficed, you made dozens and hundreds—fish, birds, trees, flowers, people. Even more amazing and wonderful is how gracious you are to give me the pleasure of living in this vast storehouse of your treasure. What a joy it is to consider all that your hands have made! "Day speaks eagerly to day, and night to night declares your praise." And everywhere I look, I see human beings of every description, as diverse as seven billion individuals can be, yet all made by you as your images, to display some unique aspect of your greatness. And wonder of wonders, I can be an agent for the extension of your holiness to them. By your sanctifying work I can become a channel that won't pollute your blessings as they flow through me into your world. May I always live so that those who experience the good I do, see that its one and only source is you. Amen and amen.

Praise for the Helper

"Ah Eternal Lord! Behold, you made the heavens and the earth by your great power and by your outstretched arm! Nothing is too difficult for you." ... "Behold, I am the Eternal, the God of all flesh; is anything too difficult for me?" Jeremiah 32:17, 27

"Here I raise my 'Ebenezer,' hither by Thy help I've come." From Egypt to Calvary, from Mizpah to Ephesus you have delivered your people from danger and death, from difficulty and disaster. No obstacle was too great for your might. No foe was too creative or resourceful for your wisdom. Neither army nor angel, neither enemy nor environment has succeeded against your people, because you intervened, because you stepped in to rescue them. For hundreds of years you strengthened faith, purified hearts, encouraged risk, and built integrity by your marvelous and glorious rescues. Today, as I remember all you have done, I am convinced of your great love. I am convinced of your mercy and grace and your eagerness to help those who cry to you, who obey your command to call on you in the day of trouble, so that you will rescue them, and they will honor you. Because of your ability to help the hopeless and to judge the wicked, I will not fear what the godless fear. You shall be my fear, and you shall be my dread; so I shall take refuge in you through the cross, and find sanctuary in Jesus' gracious, hopeful fellowship. Amen.

Praising Guidance

If you give yourself to the hungry and satisfy the desire of the afflicted, then your light will rise in darkness, and your gloom like midday. And the Lord will continually guide you, and satisfy your desire in scorched places. Isaiah 58:11

Faithful Father, you have made it so clear how you want me to live. You have shown me your glory through your grace, and you have told me of the joy I will find as I graciously extend this goodness to others. I know you know me well, for you compensate for my limitations, and gently nudge me to keep me walking along the path of life. Even when I am dull of hearing, you do what is necessary to wake me up and get my attention focused on you again. I am well known to you. You counsel me with your eye on me. You use your Spirit, the written words of Scripture, and the emotionally intense encounters with fellow believers to guide the changes in my life. How comforting it is to be certain of your careful concern. How encouraging it is to have such wisdom and insight close at hand, so I won't walk into Satan's traps. The riches of your kindness, forbearance and patience in Christ lead me to repentance. The promises guaranteed in him lead me to faith. The answers to prayer in his name lead me to continue to follow your life-giving, joy-producing guidance. How wonderful to be his disciple! Amen.

Praising Goodness

On the glorious splendor of your majesty, and on your wonderful works, I will meditate. And all shall speak of the power of your awesome acts; and I will tell of your greatness. They shall bubble over with the memory of your abundant goodness, and shall sing joyfully of your righteousness. Psalm 145:5–7

Eternal Father, I have tasted and seen that you are good. In your word are the ways of life and joy: faith, love, honesty, mercy, humility, patience, kindness, forgiveness ... When I have followed the lead of your Spirit, I have experienced the joy and peace you promised to those who trust you. Day after day you have provided for my health and strength. You have forgiven my sins and brought me back onto the narrow way. You remained close to me when I wandered away from you. In the midst of trial and trouble you were present and active on my behalf. By your gracious activity, through the ministry of others in the Body of Christ, I have grown more mature; my faith in you and my knowledge of you are approaching unity. The gifts you gave for the common good have been very good for me. How precious is your extravagant kindness, O Lord. What a joy to drink from the river of your delights. For you are the fountain of life. Your extraordinary kindness has pursued me all the days of my life; and I am satisfied to dwell in the fellowship of your house.

Present In Praise

You are holy, inhabiting the praises of Israel. In you our fathers trusted; they trusted and you delivered them. Psalm 22:3–4

"Eternal Father, strong to save, whose arm dost still the restless wave," I confess your holiness, your infinite, unexcelled and irreplaceable worth. Before you I recognize my finitude and weakness, and my own inability to secure the good in life that I desire. But you have proved yourself to be wise, powerful and fervent as you pursued me with the grace of your goodness. You have proved yourself holy in my life. Even in the midst of conflict and loneliness you have been with me. When my heart melted like wax in the hot sun, you were there to mold me back into shape. You did not hide your face from me. As a mother weaning her child, you made me trust in you. I do not always sense you there, but I have made it through nights and days without sleep; so I know you were with me. I have survived attacks and disappointments, from enemies and even from friends; so I know you were keeping me from failing in my faith, just as you kept Peter from failing in his. Heavenly Father, thank you for making your reputation holy in my heart. Thank you for exerting your kingdom power in my part of your realm. Grant me grace to gladly do your will as the angels do, in Jesus' name. Amen.

Humility's Praise

Blessed are the poor in spirit, for the kingdom of heaven consists of these. Blessed are those who mourn, for they shall be comforted. Blessed are the meek for they shall inherit the earth. Blessed are those who hunger and thirst for righteousness, for they shall be filled. Matthew 5:3–6

O Lord, it was not because of, or in spite of, my intellect or appearance or wealth or position that you chose me. I am a vapor; you are the Eternal Breath. I am a speck of dust; you are the Weight of Glory. I am a drop in the ocean; you are the Endless Fountain. I am a creature; you are the Creator. I am sustained; you are the Sustainer. In you I live and move and have my being. You hold me together by your powerful command. If you ceased to think of me, I would cease to be. When I was dead in my trespasses and sins, you made me alive. When I was a slave to sin, you set me free. When I was a subject of the Prince of Darkness, you transferred me to the kingdom of the Light of the World. Now by the power of the Holy Spirit I destroy wicked deeds that would ruin my life. How glorious is the cross by which I was crucified to the world and the world to me! I was brought low, and you saved me. So my soul returns to its rest. For you have dealt bountifully with me. You rescued my soul from death, my eyes from tears, and my feet from stumbling. Through Jesus hear my joy. Amen.

Sustained Praise

Cast your burden on the Eternal, and he will sustain you; he will never permit the righteous to be moved. Psalm 55:22

Most mighty God, by your wisdom and power you laid the foundations of the earth. The pillars of the earth are yours and on them you have built the world. Forests and glades, mountains and plains, rivers and seas were grown and shaped and guided by your skillful hand. The fullness of the world is your glory, and all of it together cries "Holy!" Day unto day and night unto night, the creation pours forth praise as you sustain its extravagant richness. You satisfy with sun and wind and rain so that the sands of the sea and the dust of the earth confirm the detail of your design. The earth rests firmly and confidently in your hand. No one but you can shake it. No one but you can shake us either. Because you are at our right hand, we have not been, nor will we ever be, shaken. Therefore our hearts rejoice and our flesh dwells secure. It has not been by our might that we prevail, but you have guarded our feet along the path. Tired, weary, lost and afraid we have faced mountainous obstacles and wondered where we would get help to cross them. Our help has come from you, maker of heaven and earth. For you who sustains the weight of the universe, our burdens are nothing. You have carried them and us with ease. When our flesh and our hearts have failed, you have been our strength. When the flight of our faith has faltered you have renewed our wings like the eagles and caused us to dance on the mountains like gazelles. For all your sustaining grace we give this praise in name of the One through whom all grace abounds. Amen

Praises of Integrity

God built his sanctuary like the heights, like the earth which he has founded forever. He also chose David his servant, ... to shepherd Jacob his people, and Israel his inheritance. So he shepherded them according to the integrity of his heart, and guided them with his skillful hands. Psalm 78:69–72

Father, you created in order to manifest your glory, and declared that the knowledge of your glory will fill the earth, as the waters cover the sea. You oversaw the dispersion of the genetic lines of Adam and Eve, so that at the right time Jesus would be born of a virgin to die in the place of your chosen people from every tribe and tongue and nation of earth, to the praise of your glory. You have never wavered in your righteous commitment to display the fullness of your glory. Even our fallible leaders are evidence of your integrity in this matter. In the Trinity there is no division. Father, Son and Holy Spirit rejoice with one joy and work together with one purpose. Jesus came and accomplished your will as though he were at a banquet. By maintaining your own integrity, you have encouraged me to maintain mine. The Spirit now gives me a heart that delights in following your way. He causes me to obey your commands with the same joy Jesus did. He enables me to know the certainty of your promises to those whose way is one with yours. The darkness recedes as the light of your glorious day spreads through my life. You are indeed the great ONE! Amen.

Mentoring Praise

As a nursing mother tenderly cares for her own children, so we, because we had so fond an affection for you, were well-pleased to impart to you not only the gospel of God but also our own lives, for you had become very dear to us. 1 Thessalonians 2:7–8

Heavenly Father, just as you gave us mothers to delight in us, to feed us, and to pour their lives into us so we would grow and flourish as human beings, you gave us parents in the faith who performed the same function. Apart from these selfless, affectionate, gracious men and women, we would have floundered not flourished. Without all the energy they poured into us, we would have died in our spiritual infancy, abandoned to the attacks of the Evil One, the appetites of the flesh and the appeal of the world. Without the precious, nourishing words of the Gospel of Jesus Christ, our souls would hunger and thirst with no hope of satisfaction. Without their care the worries of the world, the deceitfulness of material success and the desires for other sources of joy would have choked the life from our hearts. Without their protection, the heat of persecution and the anguish of affliction would have caused our souls to melt. But your proxies, your mentors, your pastor-teachers, shielded us and pruned us and refocused our attention on your glory, so that we not only survived, but thrived and have hope of bearing much glorious fruit. Now to you who can keep us from stumbling, and can make us stand in the presence of your glory blameless with great joy, be glory, majesty, dominion and authority, before all time and now and forever. Amen

The Praise of Patience

He will bring forth your righteousness as the light, and your judgment as the noonday. Therefore rest in the Eternal and wait patiently for him. Psalm 37:6

O wise and gracious God, every moment of my life comes from you. You have woven the tapestry of my days with infinite care and skill. The colors of my life are not a wash of random hues, but a precise pattern of contrasting and complementary living threads. Sometimes it seems that some of the colors will ruin the final product. So I look at some of the other beautiful lives you have woven and my willingness to wait returns. My patience is my praise of you. I want you to know that I trust you to do good to me with all your heart and soul. I want you to know that I trust you to cause all things to work together for good, that which is ideally suited to my well-being and the manifestation of your glory. I want you to know that I trust you to turn stumbling blocks into stepping stones. So I rest in you and try to respond to problems by extending the grace you have given me to my antagonists. I rest in you and try to wait for you to fulfill your promises. Jesus was patient with me. You keep allowing me time to repent, to experience more of your mercy. As I learn to trust you more and more, may the Spirit bring about longsuffering and patience in me. Amen.

Praised by Servants

Whoever serves, let him do so by the strength which God supplies; so that in all things God may be glorified through Jesus Christ, to whom belongs the glory and dominion forever and ever. 1 Peter 4:11

Over a billion people around the world, millions across the nation, thousands in my state, and hundreds in my community serve one another in the name of Jesus. You dispense extravagant gifts to them, place them in just the right place to use these gifts, and empower them through your Spirit so their gifts will be employed in just the right way to bring about the growth you had in mind. You gave the word that comforted the dying, and the gospel witness that brought life to the dead. You stirred the hearts of those who supported missionaries, and opened the eyes of those who went to reap your harvest. You guided Dorcas' hands, gilded Apollos' tongue, and guarded Timothy's ministry. Courage and vision, inspiration and hope, wisdom and love abound among your people as they serve. Best of all, you gave us One who came not to be served, but to serve. A master minister. A marvelous mentor. He took the form of a servant, challenged us to follow his example, and convinced us that just as you were with him, showing him what to do, so he would be with us, teaching us how to imitate the Only God who works for those who wait for him. Amen.

Strong Praise

Blessed be the Eternal, because he has heard the voice of my supplication. The Eternal is my strength and my shield; my heart trusts in him, and I am helped. Therefore my heart exults, and with my song I shall thank him. Psalm 28:6–7

Every experience I have with you, O God, in some way teaches me of your strength and my weakness. Because of you I live and move. You brought me into being by your command, and you hold the atoms of my body together by your powerful word. So there is no room to "esteem man, in whose nostrils is the breath of life." You have fitted me for my tasks in life, girding me with strength. You make my feet like the feet of deer that walk the mountain trails. You train me for the battle until I can "bend a bow of bronze." You strengthen my under-standing and undergird my resolve, so I can make choices that honor you and bring your grace into others' lives. And in all this you give me the "joy of a strong man running a race." More wondrously still, I know "the surpassing greatness of his power toward me the believer, which accords with the working of the strength of his might which he brought about in Christ, when he raised him from the dead, and seated him at his right hand." You answer me from your holy heaven, with the saving strength of your right hand. "Some boast in chariots, and some in horses; but I will boast in the name of the Eternal, my God," through Jesus Christ, my Lord. Amen.

Successful Praise

God saw all that he had made, and behold, it was very good. ... God blessed the seventh day and sanctified it, because in it he rested from all his work which he had created. Genesis 1:31; 2:3

O God our Creator, we work in your rest. Because you were satisfied with all that you had done, we are able to do. Because you succeeded, we can pursue success in every area of our lives. Fitting all the pieces precisely was "very good." Now we are confident of a stable and reasonable environment in which to work out what it means to be created in your image. Oh, that seventh day is so very valuable to us! And even more we value the first day of the week. For you sanctified that day by finishing an even greater work, by creating a more magnificent success. You delivered up your Son because of our sin, and raised him because of our justification. You overcame every obstacle to your plan. The nothing of pre-existence did not stop you, and the hideousness of our sin did not deter you, from realizing the accomplishment of your dream. Now as you work for those who wait for you, the final goal comes into view. Daily you sanctify every child and draw us closer to the time when we will be able to experience the fullness of what you created us to know: the wonder of your glory seen through the millions of kindnesses that come to us through Jesus Christ our Lord. Amen.

Praised for Wisdom

"Behold, the days are coming," declares The Eternal "When I shall raise up for David a righteous Branch. He will reign as king and act wisely, doing justice and righteousness in the land." Jeremiah 23:5

So often, O Lord, I celebrate your mighty acts, but today your wisdom fills my soul. In the fullness of time you left your throne and the glory of Heaven to take on human flesh so I could have both a redeemer and a role model. You showed me how one made in the image of God could display your glory by a life of faith. You glorified him fully by giving your life to deliver me from the kingdom of darkness and transfer me into the kingdom of light. What wonderful love that moved you to use your wisdom to work out a way to remain righteous while you justified the ungodly. Now I anticipate your return and the establishment of your rule here on earth. What a joy to look forward to integrity and honor in high places! What a pleasure to consider that disagreements will be resolved graciously! What a delight to think that every aspect of our society can be openly oriented to the experience of God's grace! For by your wise rule, you will make it so. Now to him who is able to establish me according to the gospel—the preaching of Jesus Christ—to the only wise God, through you, O Christ, be glory forever. Amen.

Team Praise

There are varieties of gifts, but the same Spirit; and there are varieties of service, but the same Lord; and there are varieties of activities, but it is the same God who empowers them all in everyone. 1 Corinthians 14:4–6

Together everyone accomplished more. Together you create and sustain all that is not God. Together you revealed your comprehensive plan to manifest the fullness of your glory for the joy of your people. For all of eternity, as Father, Son and Holy Spirit, you have worked with one uniting purpose so that no obstacles were able to stand in the way of expressing your delight in your own glory. Now that you've placed us in the Body of Christ, we marvel even more at the perfect coordination of your efforts. There is no conflict for credit, no fighting over favorites, only unified commitment to the final success of your plan. When you bring us onto the team, your teamwork is even more evident. Knowing all the needs of the entire Body of Christ, Holy Spirit, you manifest yourself in as many ways as are necessary to meet those needs; and Lord, you direct each of its members to be in the right place at the right time for those manifestations to be appropriately discerned; and Father, you empower each one sufficiently for each task. How glorious to see such teamwork displayed for our instruction and encouragement; how humbling to be a member of such an excellent team! Amen.

Considered Praise

One generation shall praise your works to another, and shall declare your mighty acts. On the glorious splendor of your majesty, and on your wonderful works, I will meditate. Many shall speak of the power of your awesome acts, and I will tell of your greatness. Psalm 145:4–6

Glorious God, elegant design and exquisite detail characterize the creation you spoke into being and sustain by the power of your word. For thousands of years flora and fauna have flourished according to the instructions you devised and introduced into each interconnected species. Throughout human history you intervened so we might continue to experience your goodness, keeping us from destroying ourselves in the process. You did not leave us without a witness. Regardless of how evil we became, you retained a remnant who followed you in the obedience of faith. Even more, you opened our eyes to discover the rules that govern creation, so we can manage it wisely and beneficially. But best and most amazing of all, you sent your Son to deliver me from the penalty and power of the sin which kept me from enjoying the glory of your work. By wisely using your power, the infinite God took on human form and received my punishment. You raised him from the dead, and, because of your love for him, drew millions to worship you in his name. In this brilliant light, I discern and delight in the glorious splendor of all your other deeds. Hallelujah!

Controlled for Praise

O Eternal, who may abide in your tent? Who may dwell on your holy hill? Those who walk with integrity, work righteousness, and speak truth in their hearts. They do not slander with their tongue, nor do evil to a neighbor, nor take up a reproach against a friend. Psalm 15:1–3

Fellowship with you is most precious, O God. There is no better place to be than in your presence; no better activity than engaging in conversation about you with others who love your glory. I will magnify your grace, rehearsing countless times my experience of the overflow of your joy. I will applaud your wisdom and extol your power. For you have used these not only to maintain yourself as a God worthy of worship, but also to work in my life since the day of my conception. To have fellowship with you, Father, is to delight in you as the Son does, to agree with your purpose as the Son does, and to extend your goodness as the Son does. It is worthy of all my love, loyalty, confidence, patience, and effort. I would rather be with you, humbly receiving gifts from your hand, than experiencing the short-lived thrill of self-exaltation that comes from maligning and defaming those around me. No self-created position of prominence compares with the glory of walking side by side with the Creator of the Universe. Controlling my tongue in my human relationships now is a small price to pay for the pleasure of knowing and praising your glory forever, through Jesus my Lord.

Wisdom Praised

The wisdom from above is first pure, then peaceable, gentle, reasonable, full of mercy and good fruits, unwavering, without hypocrisy. James 3:17

Heavenly Father, if wisdom were not with you from the beginning, you would not be the God I love and trust. But your wisdom caused you to delight fully in using your infinite power to be just the sort of God who is most pleasing to yourself and to me. In love, you used your wisdom to devise a way to save me from my sin, satisfy your justice, and righteously uphold your glory. What a delight it is to receive such wisdom from you! What a joy to receive from you the ability to foresee what will give me the greatest happiness for all of eternity! What a pleasure to have the capacity to relate to other men and women according to your design for our lives, to experience together the diversity of your grace and mercy. Even more amazing, you have made such wisdom so readily available to me. It is everywhere I look in Scripture. It is obvious in the complex interaction of your creation. It comes through your Spirit in answer to prayer. I can't turn anywhere, encounter any situation, or engage any cultural force, without having it immediately available. Your ways are right, O Lord, and right before my eyes. They are manna for my heart, enough for every day. Amen.

Future Praise

Though the fig tree should not blossom, nor fruit be on the vines, the produce of the olive fail and the fields yield no food, the flock be cut off from the fold and there be no herd in the stalls, yet I will exult in the Eternal; I will rejoice in the God of my salvation. Habakkuk 3:17–18

Sovereign God, you never disappoint, you never fail, your promises never fall. Though Noah waited a hundred years for rain, he built the ark in joyful anticipation of your salvation. Expectation of your saving grace kept Abraham and Sarah laughing together in love as they awaited Isaac's birth. Seven years of living in Judean caves did not dam the flow of David's joyful singing as he waited to occupy Israel's throne. Today we know only a portion of the redemption that you have promised. The fig tree of love does not blossom as often as we would like; the fruit of the Spirit does not appear abundantly on the vines of our lives. The olive branch of peace often fails in our families and among the nations. Fields are white for harvest, but the crop of faith remains small. But we know Jesus died and rose from the dead. In his resurrection we have hope. Though distressed now by various trials, we rejoice in faith. Though we have not seen him, we love him; though we do not now see him, we entrust our future to him; we rejoice with a joy inexpressible and full of glory. For in him we anticipate the experience of the glory of the riches of your grace forever. Amen!

Pleasing Praise

By faith Enoch was taken up so that he did not see death, and he was not to be found because God took him up. For before his removal he had been commended as having pleased God. Hebrews 11:5

Gracious God, pleasing you is such a pleasure! You have made it so simple. Creation reveals your wisdom and power, inviting us to understand the fullness of your glory and the greatness of your joy. Your extravagant kindness convinces us of your holiness: your infinite, unexcelled and irreplaceable worth. The cross and resurrection of Jesus demonstrate your absolute righteousness and guarantee the fulfillment of all your promises. You offer an eternity of happy tomorrows filled with marvelous surprises. What could be more reasonable than to entrust our future to you, day by day, year by year, forever? What could be more pleasurable for us or more pleasing to you? Even though we are more like Peter whose faith floundered, than like Enoch whose faith flourished, we rely on Jesus to intercede for us and on you to honor his sacrificial love; for trusting you for mercy is as pleasing to you as trusting you for everything else. So we do not worry when we are weary; we do not fear when we are frail. With Abraham we stand beneath the star-filled sky and replant our mustard seed of faith, listening in our hearts to hear again, "That's right!" and feel your pleasure drive our remaining doubts away. Yes, "it is good to sing praises to you, O God; for it is pleasant and praise is becoming." Amen.

Final Praise

Behold, this is our God; we have waited for him, that he might save us. This is the Eternal; we have waited for him; let us be glad and rejoice in his salvation. Isaiah 25:9

Hallelujah! Salvation belongs to you, O God who sits on the throne, and to the Lamb! As true worshipers we worship you, Father, in spirit and truth, for you sought us for such worship. While we were enemies you reconciled us to yourself by the death of your Son. Much more, now that we are reconciled, shall we be saved by his life. You saved us from the penalty of our sin. And now, by your Spirit, you are saving us from the power of the sin in us. And you protect us by your power through faith for a salvation ready to be revealed in the last time. You have not turned away from doing good to us. Indeed, you put fear of you in our hearts, so we will not turn from you. Worthy are you, O Christ, for by your blood you ransomed people for God from every tribe and language and people and nation, and you have made us a kingdom and priests to our God, so we will one day reign on the earth. The salvation and the power and the kingdom of our God and your authority as his Christ will come, for our accuser, who accuses us day and night before our God, will be thrown down. Satan may be sifting us, but you are saving us; and greater are you in us than he who is in the world. Together we cry, "Hallelujah! Salvation belongs to our God!"

Thanksgiving 1986

Our hearts abound with grateful joy and praise;
For you have showered mercy on our days;
And nights have come and gone with no dread fear
Inside, but peace and rest, for you were near.
In you we live and move and have our life,
In joy and sorrow, unity and strife;
From your kind hand flows all we are and claim:
Our strength to work, salvation in your name.
O Lord, our thanks today can just reflect
A portion of the joy your gifts perfect.
The beauty of your glory barely shines
Through words that come from dull and simple minds.
But words are from our hearts and thus are true:
Thank you! Thank you! Thank you! Thank you! Thank you!

Thanksgiving 1991

We weave this tapestry of thanks and praise
With words of joy that intertwine to raise
The glory of your goodness to its height,
Its beauty and its wonder in our sight.
Across the fabric, threads of golden hue
Recall your faithfulness, your love so true
That every trial bears the blessing's mark:
The light of hope that guides us through the dark.
And down the warp hang multi-colored strands.
Each shade bespeaks the skill of your deft hands:
Adroit and clever, wise beyond our dreams,
You grant us grace that circumvents our schemes.
This tapestry's a mirror that magnifies
The One who gives, the One who satisfies.

Thanksgiving 1992

From joy to joy, from grace to gratitude;
From Heaven's bounty flows beatitude.
A stream of goodness pure and deep and wide
Pours down to where we needy ones abide.
Your holiness—joy's spring and fountainhead—
Eternal excellence and worth, have led
Us eagerly to drink and realize
The glories and the wonders you devise.
With each good gift we realize anew
The greatness of the joy we have in you;
From grace to gratitude, our hearts expand
With gladness as your goodness floods the land.
So thanks stream forth in mercy and in praise,
From joy to joy, we emulate your ways.

Thanksgiving 1993

How empty, barren, desolate; devoid
Of any hope of good to be enjoyed;
How sorrowful, how pitiful the day,
If you withhold the gifts you send our way.
How cold and lonely, mis'rable; forlorn
Of comfort; little solace to be borne;
How deep, how dark, the friendless night,
If you withhold the gifts that give us light.
But you, O Gifting God, do not withhold;
Both night and day our weary eyes behold
Extravagance and lavishness in grace
Poured out upon our helpless, fallen race.
You gave your Son, by highest heaven adored;
We thank you now, through Jesus Christ, our Lord.

Thanksgiving 1994

Within our hearts, O God, we know your love
To be the greatest pleasure life can hold.
No other joy can make us rise above
Our fearfulness and cause us to be bold.
Without your gracious working on our part
We'd have no joy at all, no hope, no rest.
Without the beauty of your loving heart,
We'd never know or have the very best.
So on this day we celebrate your grace.
We set aside this time to seek your face
In humble gratitude and heart felt praise,
Remembering the glory of your ways.
O gracious Lord, we thank you from our heart
For every gift you lovingly impart.

Thanksgiving 1995

Profound, intense and undeniable,
The joy of gratitude explodes from hearts
Attuned to all the good your love imparts
As precious gifts so indescribable.
Though perfect thanks is unachieveable
While time and sin still play their foolish parts,
The glory of your holiness imparts
Desires to speak the unrestrainable
For life and love we sing exultantly;
Forgiveness when we've sinned bears joyful tears;
And answered prayer surprises and delights.
Your love approaches us triumphantly
With grace that overcomes our deepest fears
And raises our poor souls to Heaven's heights.

Thanksgiving 1996

We know your name, O Lord. We know your name;
We know your reputation and your fame.
We know your wisdom, power, love and grace;
We know your tender care and fond embrace.
We know your patience with our worst mistakes.
We know your discipline for goodness' sake;
We know you're never taken by surprise;
We know you never need to improvise.
Though chaos seems to dominate our days
And cover all your grace with murky haze,
Our gratitude will clear the mist away;
So we say, "Thanks," and celebrate today
The gracious gifts that fuel our love's bright flame.
We know your name, O Lord. We know your name.

Thanksgiving 1997

2 Corinthians 9:10–15

Though helping hands extended lovingly,
Oft bind our lives together gratefully;
And gracious words expressed in time of need,
Yield gratitude from every tiny seed;
Sometimes such deeds of love do not excite
Appreciation, pleasure or delight;
And aptly spoken words do not give rise
To joyful hearts or happy, sparkling eyes.
The miracle of giving thanks takes place
Among the ones whom God has saved by grace;
Their love is marked by liberality
That magnifies the Lord's vitality
Beyond the joy that causes praise to lift
Their hearts in thanks for giving and for gift.

Thanksgiving 1998

Our sinful, separated, lonely lives
Were changed by Jesus' gracious sacrifice;
Connected by his love the race survives
By making choices worthy of the price.
"Christ's death secured the promise of God's grace,
And in his life we see the way that's best."
By spoken word and songs our hearts embrace;
The struggling saints who hear are richly blessed.
We are identified as Jesus' own;
His name is ours to hallow or to smear.
Our speech and acts are by his grace alone,
Because the Father holds his name most dear.
Now hear, O God, our special thanks today
For grace and peace. In Jesus' name we pray.

Thanksgiving 2002

Psalm 92:1–4

No day goes by, O God, that isn't full of you:
Strong wisdom's work makes all your dreams come true
Through deeds that gladden godly hearts with good
And plant the seeds that lead to gratitude.
From early morning's grey-pink quietness
When dawn illuminates our neediness,
The promise of your grace deserves our praise,
A conscious, grateful "Thanks!" to start our days.
As night's quiescent blackness overlays
The busyness of life with temporal haze,
Our hearts see clearly all the faithful care
That warrants grateful praise beyond compare.
Since goodness grows as thanks proceeds in praise,
We thank you, Lord, for all our grace-filled days.

Thanksgiving 2003

Jeremiah 31:31–34

Your gracious covenant set forth a life
Heroic in extravagant delight:
Prosperity to make the future bright,
Security from enemies and strife.
No husband ever loved so mean a wife
Who broke the covenant in foolish spite,
Forsaking love to make herself look bright,
By cutting all her ties with pride's dread knife.
Yet grace prevailed against the heart of pride
Replacing willfulness with willingness,
Implanting law in mercy-softened breasts.
Forgiveness flowed in blood from Jesus' side,
The covenant of power from his distress,
And grateful joy to all his table's guests.

Thanksgiving 2004

Ephesians 5:18–20

Our hearts are empty, Lord, until you fill
Them with the Holy Spirit's love divine,
Which then constrains us in the Father's will
To overflow with grace by his design.
The opportunities are limitless;
We lack no faithful friend or faithless foe
Whose lives don't suffer some acute distress
That would not gain from grace that we bestow.
We join two gifts, for we are doubly blest:
The fellowship of living face to face,
And, through the Spirit, all that you deem best,
United in a grateful dance of grace.
This godly gift of friendship we acclaim,
And lift our thanks, as always, in your name.

Thanksgiving 2005

1 Timothy 4:3–5

Lord, you alone made heaven's wonders rare:
The galaxies that make the dark sky bright,
Our planet's perfect, life sustaining air,
The sun to rule the day, as moon does night.
And you alone rule over our affairs:
With hands of strength and arms outstretched in grace
You touch our sinful lives to answer prayers
And cause the saved to ever seek your face.
Because your grace endures beyond time's end
Our gratitude is ever unconfined;
As we enjoy the daily good you send
Thanksgiving comes from joy and praise combined.
So now we let the grace of food induce
The joyous thanks that grateful hearts produce.

Thanksgiving 2006

Psalm 136:1–3

Mere duty does not stir your soul to move
Your will beyond necessity's demands,
For rigid obligations never prove
Themselves through graciously extended hands.
Lord God, for all eternity your heart,
So full of joy in holy fellowship,
Has overflowed with impulses to start
To share that joy in a relationship
Of generosity and love and grace
To fully satisfy the deep desires
Encountered in each member of our race.
O God, whose gracious kindness never tires,
Receive eternal gratitude and praise
As we recount the goodness of your ways.

Thanksgiving 2007

Psalm 69:30; Psalm 34:3

Lord God, whose power, love and wisdom reign
In time and space as gracious providence,
We are confronted by the evidence
That in your vast and limitless domain
The fragile human soul cannot sustain
Itself apart from an experience
Of grateful praise for your beneficence;
Thanksgiving for your goodness keeps us sane.
So gladly we salute your loving care,
Recounting grace sufficient for the day;
You have been more than generous again,
Beyond imagining, beyond compare,
Beyond our meager power to convey
The thanks that's due in Jesus' name. Amen.

Thanksgiving 2008

Psalm 107:1–2, 8-9, 22, 31–32

Eternal God, whose goodness never ends,
Whose gracious kindness evermore remains,
We live and move while your great grace transcends
The chaos human finitude disdains.
No enemy can steal our happiness
For we have been delivered from the hand
That held our souls and caused us much distress;
Secure in faith, we take a fearless stand.
Our thirsty, hungry hearts are satisfied
As we pursue the glory of your Son,
For nothing in the world has gratified
Our need for good, as he so well has done.
Secure and stable, satisfied and free,
We'll raise our thanks throughout eternity.

Thanksgiving 2009

John 13:1–17

You dined with confidence, relaxed and sure;
You sensed the Father's providential care,
Aware your mission's goal would be secure
And grace for service would be there to spare.
Without a deprecating thought you rose
To teach your friends, through one last loving act,
That godly service keeps us on our toes,
And keeps the bond that binds our hearts intact.
For those who serve are blessed with those in need
As each encounters God's sufficient grace;
One heart is cleansed of fearfulness and greed,
The other of the fear of losing face.
O Teacher true and Lord of Life above,
We give our thanks with hearts cleansed by your love.

Thanksgiving 2010

1 Timothy 4:3–5

Your word, O God, commands a perfect end;
Designed by wisdom infinite and sure,
Creation's joys do ev'rywhere extend;
Your gifts make grace and gratitude endure.
Your word, O God, commends your works with praise,
Conveys their holy traits, invites our suit;
In supplication we affirm your ways,
Revealing worth through longing and pursuit.
So gratefully we open wide our lives;
We recognize and trust your grand intent
To grant us all a person truly needs:
Relationships in which each soul revives,
And resources that make our hearts content;
For these, with joy, our gratitude proceeds.

Thanksgiving 2011

Psalm 84:11

Eternal God, your goodness never fails:
Your infinite, enduring competence
Sustains our life and over death prevails;
Your perfect joy appears as you dispense
Extravagant and useful charity
Without the slightest sense of detriment;
Your constancy is our prosperity,
Your faithfulness makes all of us content.
So for the goodness of your well-timed grace,
The glory you display as helpful aid,
The comfort, hope and strength to face
Uncertainty and darkness unafraid;
With grateful hearts, to magnify your fame,
We come with thanks and bless your holy name.

Thanksgiving 2012

Psalm 136

To you, O God, we lift a grateful voice;
For floods of goodness pour forth from your throne,
Immersing us in reasons to rejoice,
In words and deeds that point to you alone:
The fullness of the earth deserves our praise;
The heavens are awash with rare delights:
You set the glorious sun to rule our days
And splashed the moon and stars across our nights.
You've rescued us from deep and dark distress,
For your abundant kindness never ends;
The ocean of our food seems bottomless,
For your abundant kindness never ends;
So waves of thanks from grateful hearts progress,
For your abundant kindness never ends.

Thanksgiving 2013

1 Timothy 4:4

The grace of God magnificently shows
Us how completely satisfied his heart
Must be; for all the goodness he bestows
On us becomes a work of sacred art.
There is no detail insignificant,
No element too trivial to heed;
The goodness of each person, place and plant
Is clear in that it meets a certain need.
Abundant goodness is magnificent;
We see the infinite variety
In life and sense a love extravagant
And free, affecting all society.
So we, with hearts united, speak the word
Of thanks and magnify your goodness, Lord.

Thanksgiving 2014

1 Chronicles 16:8

Today we gaze into the past at all
The kindnesses extended by your grace;
The history of charity recall
To all the members of the human race:
In the beginning we were face to face
With you and walked in daily fellowship;
Then, even when we hid in sin's disgrace,
You did not sever our relationship.
You patiently exerted leadership
Preparing earth for Jesus' ministry:
With love he offered his companionship
If we would turn from self-idolatry.
So now with grateful hearts we turn to face
The future filled with portents of more grace.

Thanksgiving 2015

Genesis 1:6–10; 1 Chronicles 16:34

Primeval deeps submitted to commands
For order as you separated land and sea;
So your creations spread across the lands,
And reveled in your liberality.
Exuberant extravagance extends
The fullness of your goodness everywhere;
And ev'ry creature born today depends,
As then, upon your gracious daily care.
Rejoicing in the goodness of your grace,
We celebrate your wisdom and your might:
Each gift so suitable for time and place,
Ideally formed for our intense delight.
With all our hearts we raise our thanks today,
And bless you for the goodness you display.

Thanksgiving Sonnet 2016

Psalm 97:9-12; 1 John 1:5–7; 2:8

O God of everlasting life, your light
Illuminates the world so we might scan
With panoramic vision what is right
And good and fits in with your perfect plan.
With light comes gladness for the upright heart;
We walk with you in utter confidence
That you will guard our souls and do your part
To keep us living in obedience.
For Jesus Christ has come to your defense,
So you can justly cast our sin away
And welcome us as children to your side.
With grateful hearts we bless your excellence;
Our thanks for all the love that you display,
The infinite abundance you provide.

Christmas 1982

For years you overlooked our insolence
Wherein we praised ourselves and did not heed
Your gracious offers of beneficence,
Nor give you thanks for meeting our great need.
We heaped up scorn on your delightful gift,
And walked instead our own rebellious path;
So that our independence caused a rift
That held but promise of your sudden wrath.
Yet that is not your ultimate desire;
For Jesus' birth shows wisdom did abound
And find a way for love to quench wrath's fire,
Ensuring all the while your glory would resound.
O make your glory shine in our dark hearts
So we might know the peace his birth imparts.

Christmas 1983

Anticipation of your birth ran high
Two thousand years ago, as angels stood
With trumpets raised to sound the joyous cry
That God at last would make his promise good.
For Christ the Lord of heav'n and earth would come
And dwell with men to save them from God's wrath,
And make available the Spirit: Sum
Of all God's joy, and light for life's dark path.
Emmanuel, the mighty Son of God,
Restorer of creation's grand design,
That earth be filled with images of God,
Who shed abroad his glory through their line.
O let us, as your angels did above,
Feel joy and wonder at the glory of your love.

Christmas 1984

O Christ, you came to share with Abram's seed
The tempting faced by each in time of need.
No suffering moved you to be afraid;
You called yet more upon the Father's aid.
For every threat to happiness you sensed,
You trusted to God's knowing providence.
The fear of death did not enslave your soul
For you were freed by trusting God's control.
So when you died to sin upon the tree
You made this freedom possible for me:
My sinful fears were covered to God's sight,
And Satan's pow'r o're death has lost its might.
With joy, O Christ, we celebrate your birth,
With gladness your nativity on earth.

Christmas 1985

We celebrate your coming down to earth,
Rejoicing that one reason for your birth
Was all the joy you had in heav'n above,
The joy that overflowed to us in love.
We celebrate your coming, Holy One,
To save us from God's wrath for sins we've done,
And give us hearts that long to glorify
Our great creator God, who lives on high.
We celebrate your coming Jesus, Lord.
O gift of God who as our heart's reward
Fulfills our need for pleasure and for love.
Our joy becomes like that of heav'n above.
Your grace, sweet Jesus, shines in our dark night;
Let us reflect the glory of your light.

Christmas 1987

In God on high, whose glory knows no end,
Eternal majesty and mercy blend.
Divine omnipotence and wisdom bind
Together righteousness for all mankind.
Dark fear invades our souls each time we see
The glory of the holy Trinity.
The sinful hearts of earth need grace
So we can kneel in joy before his face.
In sovereign freedom Heaven's Lord descends:
Becomes for us the sinner who offends.
Bestows his grace and opens wide our eyes,
So we can love what truly satisfies.
Good news! Great joy is here for us on earth;
Salvation! Peace with God, by Jesus' birth.

Christmas 1988

The angel sang good news, "Great joy for earth!
O go to Bethlehem, and see the Savior's birth!
The Lord on high has glorified his name.
A light for all the nations is aflame."
By river's edge, illumined by that light,
A purple seller's darkened heart turned white.
Rejoicing brought about obedience.
For Jesus' name had given confidence.
The windows of his light refused to close.
Instead loud songs of loving praise arose.
The babe of Bethlehem broke down the wall.
His glory brought the jailer's heart in thrall.
Still shines the light revealing God's great love.
Now hopes the heart illumined from above.

Christmas 1990

Jeremiah 32:17; Isaiah 7:9–14; Luke 1:37

O God of heaven and earth, of skies and deeps,
We see with joy what your word made and keeps.
There is no work too wondrous for your hand,
No obstacle to hinder your command.
Your promises of old deserve belief;
No child who trusts will know eternal grief.
And wondrous signs are given for our aid,
To strengthen fearful hearts and to persuade.
Twice-told, the promise of the virgin made
The hope of what it signified displayed
With glory great enough to bring about
Our wonder, adoration most devout.
It proved, the Son's nativity so odd,
That nothing is impossible with God.

Christmas 1992

Matthew 12:15–21; Luke 18:19–20; Hebrews 12:1

From all the corners of the land they came,
The dumb, the blind, the beggars and the lame.
Each one came seeking Jesus' special touch.
They found the King whose power changed so much.
From prisons of the mind and heart they poured,
The lonely and the guilty and the bored.
Each one sensed freedom in the Savior's word.
They found that joy with Jesus as their Lord.
So each of us from every walk of life,
Who saw a world of suffering and strife,
We all joined in the search for hope and love.
Our Master gave his Spirit from above.
Community of holiness and grace,
A team to help each other run The Race.

Christmas 1993

Humility's the crown God wore the day
He sent his Son to take our sins away.
It circled round his condescending head,
As cloth and straw became the child's bed.
Below his crown the robe of meekness trailed
Across the glory sinners have assailed.
On earth the Son's proclaimed by shepherds' mean
Announcements as they wander from the scene.
God reigns; his scepter sovereignly extends
In wisdom to the holy child's friends:
A tender staff goes forth to goad and guide
Each sheep that wanders from the Shepherd's side.
Some day this humble, meek and tender grace
Will bring God's joy to every heart and face!

Christmas 1994

Incarnate deity surprised the world.
So unexpecting people blindly swirled
Around his birth, and missed creation's king
As he arrived to take away death's sting.
The little babe lay helpless in the straw.
So no one knew how angels watched in awe
As God's great mystery of love began
To be revealed according to his plan.
Though twenty hundred years have slipped away,
It seems that very few can see today
That Jesus really was God's holy Son
And Mankind's loving savior all in one.
Almighty, wise and ever gracious Lord,
Reveal yourself through sinners you've restored.

Christmas 1995

Encased in guilt and chained to sin's dark way,
The world in hopeless dread of judgment lay,
Until the angel shouted out the news
That Heaven's God would pay earth's righteous dues.
In ignorance and shadow joy was bound;
Deceitful promises—just empty sound;
Then glory knifed like lightening through the sky
As God released the Truth that slew the lie.
With Jesus comes the reconciling deed
That makes all God's good promises succeed:
Forgiveness, peace, and hope bring purest joy;
God frees us from our sin through Mary's boy.
Angelic choirs once sang of grace to come;
But we will sing of grace that brought us home!

Christmas 1999

Romans 3:25–26; 1 Timothy 1:15–16; 2 Peter 3:9

Long suffering from human wickedness—
His gracious love and helpful hand ignored—
Yet God did not reveal his righteousness
In wrath because he was not lovingly adored.
Forbearance of this painful ignorance
Caused doubt to grow in sinful human souls:
"Are we just subject to the tides of chance,
Or is his patience working toward his goals?"
Christ Jesus came at last to demonstrate
How patient mercy from the Lord was right:
The sinners' punishment he took was great.
True Christmas gift to all who are contrite,
Longsuffering has brought us to our knees;
Salvation from the patient Prince of Peace.

Christmas 2000

We come, O Christ of Christmas, to a hall
To celebrate with friends your timely birth;
Now one event divides the years for all
The peoples, tribes and languages of earth.
We come, O Christ of Christmas, to a meal
To strengthen hearts and souls by your good grace;
The gifts of God receive their righteous seal
Because you came to join the human race.
We come, O Christ of Christmas, to a time
When thoughts of light and love and joy abound;
Despair and gloom give way to hope sublime
That peace will blanket all the world around.
So come, O Christ of Christmas, come again,
And rid the world of sadness and of sin.

Christmas 2001

John 1:14–18

O Word of God, Incarnate Deity,
You dwelt among the lowly human race.
Embodiment of heaven's piety,
No glory matches yours for truth or grace.
Unseen, the Father lives from day to day
Unknowable to any human mind.
Yet as we watched you walk in our dark way
We understood him: faithful, pure and kind.
And from your fullness we have all received
The joyful overflow that we call grace;
Especially the grace of grace relieved
So law and love for God at last embrace.
Your excellence, O living Christmas King,
Your glory, bold with grace and truth, we sing!

Christmas 2002

2 Corinthians 1:18–20

How many are the promises God makes?
To choose his people first without mistakes;
Then join their destinies to each one's soul,
And cause the change of mind that makes them whole.
Forgiveness reconciles the faithful to his grace;
While grace prepares each child to see his face,
And keeps us as we walk along life's way
Until at last we see the glorious day.
Because Christ Jesus, God's anointed Son,
Uniquely qualified himself as one
Whose faithfulness secured the covenant,
We look to all the Father has to grant
And recommit ourselves to faith again:
To glorify his love with loud "Amen!"

Christmas 2003

1 Timothy 1:15–16

At Christmas wonder is appropriate
Because Christ Jesus left the Father's side
And came to us as an expatriate
To be the one on whom our hopes relied.
For, blackened by the sin of unbelief,
Not one of us could stand before God's face
Without receiving wrath for all the grief
We caused him when we snubbed and spurned his grace.
Yet in Christ's love a patient power rests,
So that no matter what has been our case,
He suffers long, and perfectly arrests
Sin's power to obstruct our move to grace.
Because we can depend on this true word,
We celebrate your birth with faith, O Lord.

Christmas 2005

Luke 1:35–37; Zechariah 8:6–8; Jeremiah 32:27

When obstacles appear to thwart God's grace,
We do not use the word "Impossible."
For nothing in creation can disgrace
The Lord or make his plans unfeasible.
His promises are not dismissible
Though human eyes see mountains made of pain,
And sinful failures make implausible
The hope and joy he offers to sustain.
Immutable and righteous, God must strain
To satisfy his wholly just demands;
So love moves might and wisdom to attain
For us the terms his covenant commands.
"Impossibly" the Son of God descends
And Christmas joy to all the world extends.

Christmas 2006

Isaiah 7:14; John 1:14

From Heaven's splendor God Almighty sent
To us a splendid gift: Immanuel.
As day from night is wholly different,
The Holy One arrived: Immanuel.
With gracious words he spoke defiantly
Of God's requirements: Immanuel.
Both wind and sea obeyed compliantly
While fearful men still sinned: Immanuel.
The Son of Man, according to God's plan,
Showed us the way to live: Immanuel.
The Son of God was born to us a man
So he could bear our guilt: Immanuel.
With us was God, our lives redeemed from hell;
God is with us, still our Immanuel!

Christmas 2007

Anointed "Prophet," Moses' perfect heir,
We turn to you, O Christ, as Word made flesh,
For truth and clarity. With love declare
The will of God, and our dull hearts refresh.
Anointed "Priest," untouched by human sin,
Melchizedek's apparent heir: O plead
Our case, Lord Christ. Your righteous life will win
God's heart from which forgiveness can proceed.
Anointed "King," the Branch from David's tree,
Most sovereign Christ, who reigns from heav'n above,
We look to you for life and liberty;
O keep us loyal to your law of love.
Anointed "saints," with all our hearts we sing:
We hail your glory, Prophet, Priest and King

Christmas 2009

Luke 2:9–11

"Fear not!" rang out across the countryside;
"Fear not!" rings down the years, to comfort all
Encountering the glory of God's pride
Emblazed upon our heart's dismaying pall.
Resplendent in the blackness, glory shines,
But sinful hearts recoil, amazed, afraid;
Not knowing what to make of God's designs;
By all our vain and empty boasts betrayed.
"Replace your fear with hopeful joy," he said,
"For glory points to grace, not vengeful wrath;
Salvation from your darkness lies ahead,
And glory's stream reveals your godly path."
So, as of old, we all with one accord
Go to the Savior, Jesus, Christ the Lord.

Christmas 2010

John 8:12; 12:45–46

You came into a world where people fight
To close their eyes against the light of life;
Then, stumbling in the dark, their souls excite
Themselves to vicious argument and strife.
You came into a world where darkness rules,
Where blind men say they see, and lead the blind
Onto the kind of path that only fools
With willful hearts would fail to see is mined.
You came as light into the darkling world,
Revealing God in ev'ry word and deed,
A spotlight on the glory of his worth.
You came as light into our hopeless world,
So those of us who trust you might succeed,
Might love the light ignited by your birth.

Christmas 2011

Mark 1:23–24

"The Holy One of God!" he cried in pain;
Then Jesus spoke the words that freed a soul
From bondage in the enemy's domain,
Establishing the scope of his control.
Thus God, incarnate, causes us to know
The value we should place upon his name;
There is no good that he will not bestow,
For perfect blessings lead to his acclaim.
To whom else could we go for so much grace?
In Christ the promises of God come true.
Beyond the limits placed by time and space
The goodness of God's Holy One breaks through.
So we confess with joy that we believe
The words of life, and wait for our reprieve.

Christmas 2013

Ephesians 1:5–7; 2:2–3

At Christmas time we contemplate your grace:
The fullness of your joy so lavishly
Bestowed on children wild of heart and face,
Annoyed by love, and living churlishly:
Our angry arrogance denied that we
Depend on you for daily sustenance,
That life without your gracious gifts would be
More horrible than we could countenance.
So Christmas celebrates your godly child
Who came to save us from our wrathful pride;
A meek and humble servant, filled with wild
Commitment to the grace we'd cast aside;
In whom we have redemption through his blood;
Through whom we praise your glory, gracious God.

Christmas 2014

Hebrews 2:9–18; 4:14–16

We come with confidence to seek your grace;
To find the help we need when life is hard;
We come for real mercy in the face
Of failure which has left us worn and scarred.
We come for sympathy when our hearts quail
Before a test of faith which takes away our breath;
We come for strength which fear cannot assail
Despite the certain prospect of our death.
We come because the Christ-child came to earth
To share the depth of our humanity,
The fullness of our finitude and fear.
We come in celebration of his birth,
Who overcame the worst adversity
To gain for us the life which we hold dear.

Christmas 2015

Isaiah 9:6–7

We gaze, O God, at kids when they arrive.
We stare, amazed as tiny hands and feet
Emerge into the world where they will strive
And work and strain to make their lives complete.
We think of all the effort they'll expend
To overcome the obstacles they face,
When what they really need's a royal friend
Who'll open wide for them the gates of grace.
Today we celebrate the child who came
From Jesse's root and David's family,
According to the promise in your Word,
Who'll govern justly in the Father's name,
Securing grace, for which they'll happily
Proclaim him as their everlasting Lord.